LANGSTON'S TRAIN RIDE

BY
ROBERT BURLEIGH

ILLUSTRATED BY
LEONARD JENKINS

ORCHARD BOOKS · AN IMPRINT OF SCHOLASTIC INC. · NEW YORK

To Evan Robert Burleigh, with love   — R.B.

LIBRARY OF CONGRESS CATALOGING-IN-PUBLICATION DATA

Burleigh, Robert; Jenkins, Leonard, ill.

Langston's train ride / by Robert Burleigh; illustrated by Leonard Jenkins. p.   cm.

Summary: Describes how the twentieth-century African American poet Langston Hughes affirms his

vocation as a writer through the composition of his famous 1921 poem "The Negro Speaks of Rivers."

 [1. Hughes, Langston, 1902–1967—Juvenile literature. 2. Hughes, Langston, 1902–1967. 3. Poets,

American—20th century—Biography—Juvenile literature. 4. African American poets—Biography—Juvenile

literature. 5. Poets, American. 6. African Americans—Biography.]

PS3515.U274 Z6176 2004   818/.5209 B 21   2003049899

ISBN: 0-439-35239-8

10 9 8 7 6 5 4 3 2 1   04 05 06 07 08

Printed in Singapore 46 · First edition, October 2004

The text type was set in Arbitrary Bold. Book design by David Caplan.

AUTHOR'S NOTE

I love the poetry of Langston Hughes. In *Langston's Train Ride*, I wanted to capture just one thing: the moment when Langston Hughes came to believe in himself as a writer.

The details of this moment and the wonderful poem — "The Negro Speaks of Rivers" — that he wrote that late afternoon are unique to the life of Langston Hughes. But many people have experienced something similar: the realization that they can achieve their dreams.

My hope is that *Langston's Train Ride* is not only a historic retelling but also a beacon for other young people with a dream.

— Robert Burleigh

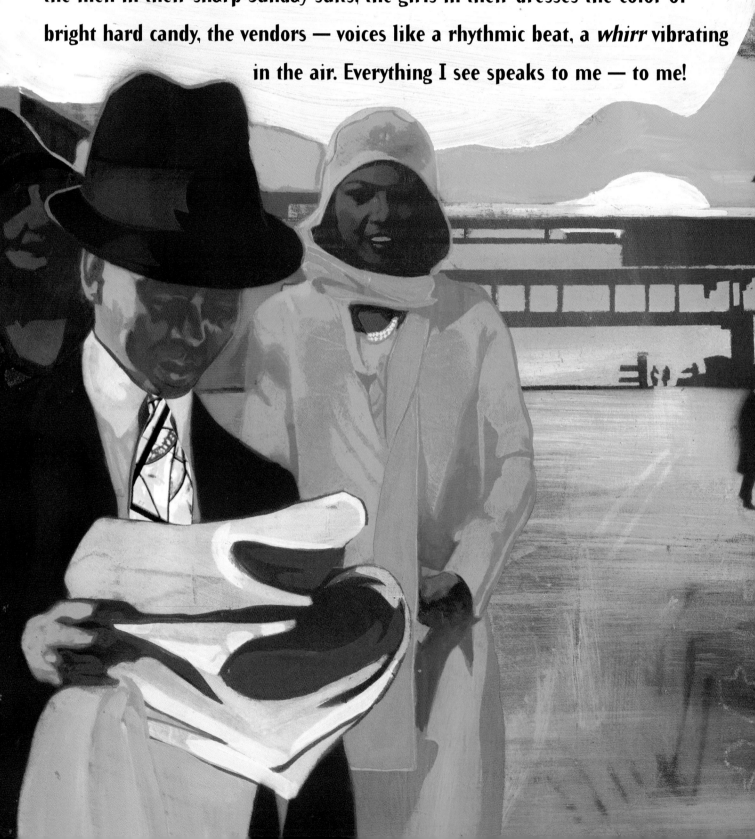

Sunday afternoon in Harlem, and 125th Street is alive, swarming with people. Jumping and jiving! I'm home! I love walking these streets — the faces, the men in their sharp Sunday suits, the girls in their dresses the color of bright hard candy, the vendors — voices like a rhythmic beat, a *whirr* vibrating in the air. Everything I see speaks to me — to me!

I'm on my way — to one of the best days of my young life. Look

out, Harlem, I'm coming through! My first book of poems —

out at last! I've got to make it to a party where all my friends

are waiting — just for me! I skit-skat a little half-dance on

the sidewalk. Yes, I am a poet! I know it now, but there was

a time when I wasn't so sure. Not so sure at all. My heels

click faster and faster on the sidewalk. That sound pulls

me back to that time not so many years ago. I drift back.

And back some more . . .

Clackety clack clack clack. Yes, I'm riding the rails! With my head tilted against the seat, I listen to the sleepy click of the train wheels, resting my feet on the steel bar in front. Happily, I gaze out at the soft blur of trees through the dust-flecked window.

It's 1920, and here I am — all of eighteen years old. High school is behind me, and I'm traveling to Mexico to visit my father, who lives there — my father, who left us to fend for ourselves when I was just a little boy.

The train rumbles south and west, bumping and swaying. Past green fields dotted with grazing horses and thin streams that dart suddenly out of the woods.

From Ohio into Indiana. Little towns with white steeples and lazy stations. Here and there, at the edge of one of these towns, the tar-paper shacks or broken-down sheds where my people — the Negro people — live.

"Start out with nothing sometime," my grandmother liked to say, "and see how long it takes to work up to something."

Riding along, I remember my grandmother, who raised me. I loved her pride. I loved her free spirit. I loved the stories she told me about her first husband, who died fighting to end slavery. (One time, she showed me his shawl full of bullet holes!)

I think of many others, too. The black men and women in my church who cared for me. My Auntie Reed, who cooked wonderful apple dumplings with butter sauce. And all the black folks I'd met while working in an ice cream parlor in Cleveland. They came north with nothing but their brave thunderclap laughter that said, "No matter what, I'll keep on going."

The train rolls on, as the sun starts setting
over endless rows of Illinois cornfields.
And then, very slowly, we're crossing
a long bridge. It's the Mississippi River,
far below, with a beautiful golden
light shimmering on it. The trees on the
farthest shore seem ablaze. Something
deep inside me stirs. I feel more awake
than I've ever been before.

Looking down on its wide, dark flow, I think of what this

river means to my people. Slaves worked here — on boats,

in nearby fields, and alongside the banks, stacking sandbags

to hold back floods. Some slaves were sent "down the river,"

too, to be worked to death on the meanest plantations.

I even remember that Abe Lincoln once traveled this river

on a raft, all the way to New Orleans, where he saw a slave

auction and learned to hate slavery.

Whoosh. Words and phrases come rushing into my head.

The names of other ancient rivers bubble up. African rivers.

The Congo. The Nile. The Euphrates.

Suddenly, three words. Just three — but I know I have to write them down. How? Where? I snatch the envelope with my father's letter in it and turn it over. Who cares where — just write! On the back side, with a little stubby pencil I always carry, I write the words:

I've known rivers.

My thoughts roam. Suddenly, I feel the history of my people flowing right up to this moment — to ME. Yes, I feel I've lived other lives on those muddy riverbanks. Somehow, somewhere, I've heard the dusky waters of all those rivers lapping and singing. It's true, it's true. I've known rivers.

I keep the envelope flat on my lap. I'm madly scribbling words down now, rapidly one after another. (Poems are like rainbows, don't you think? They escape if you're not quick!)

I turn my head to get one last look at the sun-tinged Mississippi. Going, going, gone. I scrawl the last line:

My soul has grown deep like the rivers.

And the poem is done.

Carefully, I place the envelope inside my coat pocket. Mustn't lose this, no way! I sit there, gazing at the reflection of my face in the glass, reciting the poem to myself over and over and over.

I lean forward and press my nose against the window. Everything is gathered up in one huge darkness. But as I stare out, I see a few tiny dots of light balanced on the edge of the horizon.

Questions keep coming into my head: *Am I really a poet? Is it possible? Can I sing my America, too, as other great poets have sung theirs? Can I?*

Then, as I watch the far-off, flickering lights, a very tiny voice inside me answers softly but firmly, *Yes*, it says, *yes, yes.* I settle back in my seat. The wheels hum. The car sways gently on and on. . . .

Suddenly, I hear the staccato street sounds again. A large

crowd of people is waving at me. I arrive in front of the

Shipwreck Inn. "Langston," someone shouts, "sit down and

sign some books!"

So I do, still feeling the rhythm of that long-ago train

ride under my feet. A friend calls out, "Langston, read some

poems, read some poems."

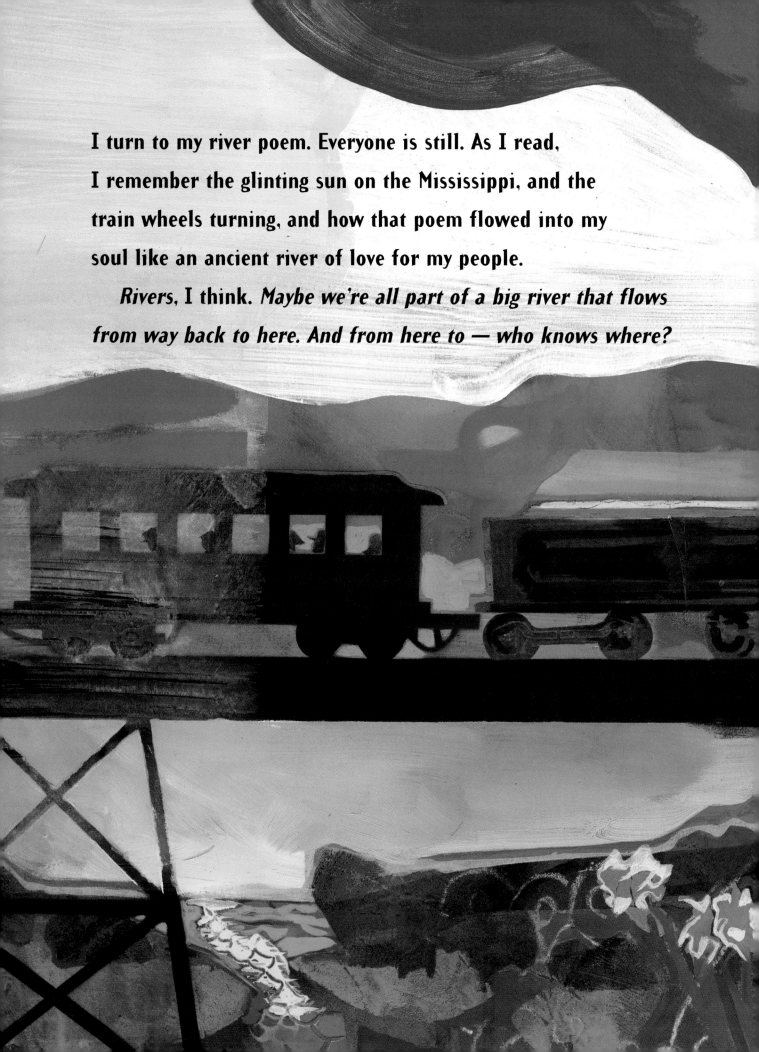

I turn to my river poem. Everyone is still. As I read,
I remember the glinting sun on the Mississippi, and the
train wheels turning, and how that poem flowed into my
soul like an ancient river of love for my people.

*Rivers, I think. Maybe we're all part of a big river that flows
from way back to here. And from here to — who knows where?*

THE NEGRO SPEAKS OF RIVERS

My soul has grown deep like the rivers.

I bathed in the Euphrates when dawns were young.

I built my hut near the Congo and it lulled me to sleep.

I looked upon the Nile and raised the pyramids above it.

I heard the singing of the Mississippi when Abe Lincoln

went down to New Orleans, and I've seen its muddy

bosom turn all golden in the sunset.

I've known rivers:

Ancient, dusky rivers.

My soul has grown deep like the rivers.

— Langston Hughes

AFTERWORD

Langston Hughes is one of America's greatest poets. He was born in Joplin, Missouri, on February 1, 1902, but grew up in several places in the Midwest, including Kansas, Illinois, and Cleveland, Ohio, where he graduated from high school in 1920. While in high school, Hughes was both class poet and a star performer in track.

Although Langston's father, who lived in Mexico, tried to discourage Langston from becoming a writer, the young man began writing and publishing poetry at an early age. One of his first and most well-known poems, "The Negro Speaks of Rivers," appeared in 1921 in the magazine *Crisis*, edited by the African-American leader W.E.B. Du Bois.

During the 1920s, Hughes spent time in New York City, where he was part of the black American literary movement known as the Harlem Renaissance. He published his first volume of poetry, *The Weary Blues*, in 1926. Many poems in this book are written in a blues, jazz, or slang style that was always one feature of his work.

As a newspaper columnist, Hughes created a very popular character named Simple, whose witty and wise pronouncements on American (and especially African-American) life appeared in newspapers for twenty-five years.

During his lifetime, Hughes received many fellowships, awards, and honorary degrees. When he died on May 22, 1967, Langston Hughes was recognized as a fighter for justice and a poet whose work would stand the test of time.